STEP UP!

Second Edition

HOW TO BE AN EXCELLENT
NONPROFIT BOARD MEMBER

ELIZABETH BAILEY

NANCY SCHMIDT

LATITUDE 33 PUBLISHING

Latitude 33 Publishing
2629 Manhattan Avenue, #306
Hermosa Beach, CA 90254

Editor: Betsey Binét
Design: Gretchen Goetz

ISBN 978-0-9907349-3-2

Library of Congress Control Number: 2019912290

Printed in the United States of America
10 9 8 7 6 5 4 3 2 1

This book is dedicated to
the individuals who step up every day
to help lead their organizations.
You are truly the embodiment of pioneering
anthropologist Margaret Mead's call:
"Never doubt that a small group of
thoughtful, committed people can change the world;
indeed, it's the only thing that ever has."

Thank you to our wonderful families, friends,
colleagues, clients and creative team for
consistently demonstrating the meaning of excellence.

STEP UP!

HOW TO BE AN EXCELLENT NONPROFIT BOARD MEMBER

Second Edition

Table of Contents

Here's to stepping up!

On the scale of doing things in your lifetime that matter, serving on a board ranks way up there.
It's an honor. And it's a tremendously important job with far-reaching implications. In fact, in *Engaged and On Board,* a national study we conducted of more than 1,200 nonprofit board members across the country, a resounding 85% agreed that their board service has helped them make a bigger impact than any other type of volunteering they have done.

Along with the great sense of satisfaction that
comes from "doing good," board members overwhelmingly identified two major personal benefits:

- 95% made important new relationships
- 92% gained new skills

And the good news for those who are joining boards is that 84% have found the experience to be even better than they had expected.

It's an honor.

And it's a tremendously

important job

with far-reaching

implications.

It's a big job. Beyond the personal rewards you may gain from board membership, you are being entrusted with a very real, very important responsibility. Your actions tangibly impact the lives of many other important people: those who work or volunteer for the organization as well as those whom the organization exists to serve.

We have been privileged to devote much of our careers to the social-change sector. The following pages contain insights we've gained from many hours in board rooms and with staff, witnessing the highs and the lows, facilitating meaningful discussions and helping to guide organizations to new levels of engagement, impact and excellence. **We hope these insights will help you make the most of your board experience.**

"**Anyone** can make a difference

and **everyone** should try."

JOHN F. KENNEDY

This is no ordinary hat.

A great way to start your board service is by appreciating that you are already in an enviable position:

- **You've found an organization you care about.**
  Maybe it's because you or someone close to you has benefited from the organization's work. Or you've gotten to know them through volunteering or donating. Or you simply admire what they stand for and how they operate. Regardless of the reasons, something about it resonates with you and you feel a connection.
- **You've been noticed.** The organization's leadership has identified you as a person who has something important to bring to the table: skills, experience, commitment, resources, connections and, of course, passion.
- **You've been invited.** And you've accepted!

From the moment you said yes, you're wearing a new hat: **Board Member**.

And that comes with a crucial mind shift.

Being on a board is not a solo journey. Rather, you're part of a team that's at the helm of the organization. It is this group's decisions that define the organization's priorities and course of action, and that help set its culture. So as a board member, you are impacting both its current operations and future success.

Sounds pretty consequential, doesn't it? It is! While you will always retain the personal motivations and perspectives that initially brought you to the board, you now have a larger responsibility – looking out for the interests of the organization as a whole.

Being a board member means that there will be times when you'll be challenged to stretch beyond the familiar. Highly effective board members wholeheartedly agree that the skills they hone and the relationships they build while serving make board membership one of the most satisfying roles they have ever taken on.

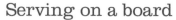

Serving on a board

is not something everyone gets to experience. It's an exceptional opportunity to make a lasting difference for a cause and an organization you believe in.

So before you put your board hat on, make sure it fits.

- Do you understand the organization's mission and fully support it?

- Have you gone to the organization's website or to an online nonprofit database such as candid.org to review the nonprofit's Form 990? (The 990 is the form that enables the IRS and the public to evaluate a nonprofit's operations.)

- Have you familiarized yourself with the other individuals who are on the board?

- Are you clear about what the expectations are for board members, and can you commit to fulfilling them?

- Are you ready for action?

Then if it looks and feels right, put on your board hat and wear it with pride!

"The strength of the team

is each individual member.

The strength of each member

is the team."

PHIL JACKSON
BASKETBALL HALL OF FAME COACH

Play your position.

When you become a board member, it's sometimes difficult to know what position you're playing. It's not your home turf. You need to know who is responsible for what, what is and isn't off limits, and how hands-on you should be.

Why you're on the team

Looking at the big picture, as a board member your goals are to:

- Make sure the organization is financially well-run and has the resources needed to fulfill its mission and goals.

- Help set high-level policy and strategy.

- Be an an informed, visible connector, advocate and supporter of the organization.

- Build and maintain a competent and engaged board.

- Protect and model the organization's core values.

- Hire and empower a skilled chief executive who builds and leads an effective staff team.

- Conduct the annual performance review for the chief executive.

Would you accept a paying job
without knowing what
was expected of you?

Of course not!
Yet, as our national study of
nonprofit organization board members
revealed, only one-third believed that
they had been fully oriented to their new role
and understood what was expected of them.

SOURCE: ENGAGED AND ON BOARD NATIONAL STUDY
Conducted by 2B Communications, 2015

What's not in your playbook

Many board members are experienced leaders, and that may be one reason you have been asked to serve. If so, you're probably used to calling the shots — deciding who will fill key roles, which products or services to offer, how to market and sell them. While your expertise is certainly valued, *running the organization is not part of your board member job description.*

That's not to say that the board is completely distanced from the workings of the organization; rather, it's that the board and the staff have their own assignments.

Know the rules of engagement

Make it a priority at the outset to become familiar with your board responsibilities, written and unwritten. Effective boards:

- Set clear board member expectations.
- Maintain a culture of accountability.
- Use data and information to guide decisions.
- Respectfully vet differences of opinion.
- Maintain confidentiality.
- Provide constructive feedback to the chief executive.

Good information leads...

to better decisions.

- **Every nonprofit should have an annual budget.** It's good practice for the board to review the budget vs. actual financial reports on a monthly basis, even if you only meet quarterly.

- **For many nonprofits, cash flow is a challenge.** Generating a monthly cash flow forecast helps to head off potential problems.

- **Running the organization is not your job.** However, management reports for key areas such as programs and fundraising help ensure that both board and staff are focused on the most important priorities.

As a starting point, there are some general baselines for what board and staff members typically do in key areas:

Operations: Staff members create the annual budget based on the overall strategic priorities of the organization, and board members approve it. From there, staff develop and implement work plans under the guidance and management of the chief executive, who supplies reports to the board. Board member responsibilities are to ensure the information they receive is thorough and sufficient, and then carry out their **specified fiduciary responsibilities.**

So what does being a fiduciary mean? In simple terms, it means being a steward of the public trust and always acting for the good of the nonprofit you're helping to lead. It also means that you're legally responsible for overseeing the nonprofit's assets. You don't have to be a financial genius, but you do need to know what questions to ask:

- Are our finances consistent with our budget and our strategic plan?
- Are our reserves adequate? (A typical nonprofit goal is 3-6 months of operating expenses, although that can vary.)
- Are our expenses and revenue in alignment with budget expectations?
- Are appropriate checks and balances in place to prevent errors or abuse?
- Are we meeting our funders' guidelines and requirements?
- Are we fulfilling our legal obligations (such as the timely and accurate filing of our Form 990, or conducting an annual audit)?

In short:

The board is the **"WHAT"**

and staff is the **"HOW"**

Big-picture goals and strategies,
not department operational plans

Overall financials and budgets,
not individual program or event line items

Whether to open or close facilities,
not the details of running the facilities

New programmatic direction,
not program staffing or management

Selecting a new name,
not art directing the new website
or marketing materials

If you're new to the financial responsibilities associated with being a board member, take the time outside of the board room to learn more about fiduciary responsibilities, including how to read the organization's financial reports and understand its business and revenue models. Typically, meeting with staff or your Board or Finance Committee Chair will help you get up to speed.

Policymaking and Strategic Decisions:

Initial ideas can come from either staff or the board; however, it's the board's job to vet and approve significant strategic changes and key policy positions using information provided by board committees, staff and/or trusted consultants. Major strategic decisions include actions such as acquiring or selling property, major facility renovations, entering into a new programmatic area, changing the organization's name, pursuing a major government contract, or forming a substantive strategic partnership. Implementation, such as designing programs, hiring personnel, preparing proposals or developing new materials, is then handled by the organization's staff.

What's the secret to a great Board Chair/Chief Executive relationship?

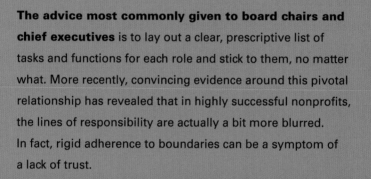

The advice most commonly given to board chairs and chief executives is to lay out a clear, prescriptive list of tasks and functions for each role and stick to them, no matter what. More recently, convincing evidence around this pivotal relationship has revealed that in highly successful nonprofits, the lines of responsibility are actually a bit more blurred. In fact, rigid adherence to boundaries can be a symptom of a lack of trust.

Research confirms that the strongest partnerships are developed through open dialogue and a flexible, ongoing process of give-and-take, in which both individuals continually learn and find ways to tap each other's unique strengths and interests, to better achieve the organization's goals.

SOURCE: STUDY BY MARY L. HILAND, PHD, 2005

Working with staff is a balancing act.

The more involved you are, the more likely you'll work directly with staff from your nonprofit. In fact, you may spend more one-on-one time working with staff on projects or committees than you do with the chief executive. And that can be tricky.

Staff are obliged to work with you in two different ways: Deferring to you as a strategic leader of the organization and, on a more practical level, giving you assignments and direction in specific areas such as fundraising. Being mindful of this duality will help you establish and maintain collaborative and productive staff relationships to ensure you get what you need to be both a leader and a doer.

What if staff have a serious complaint about the Chief Executive?

It's good practice to have a formal process that enables staff to raise concerns about major issues such as mismanagement. This can be accomplished by clearly communicating to staff that serious complaints should follow the procedures established by the nonprofit's human resources department. Typically, complaints concerning the chief executive are directed to the Board Chair, who would then choose to communicate directly with the chief executive about the issue and/or bring it to the board for further exploration.

In most organizations, when a board member calls, it triggers someone on staff to jump — sometimes really high. That can put staff members in an awkward position: As much as they may want to help, it can also distract them from the tasks for which they're being held accountable. Being thoughtful about these requests will help keep such situations in check.

As you build relationships with staff and develop mutual trust, it's imperative to remain "above board." **Some lines should never be crossed:**

- Engaging in off-the-record conversations about your fellow board members, the organization or its chief executive.
- Leveraging relationships with staff to gain an "insider scoop."
- Putting yourself in a position that could be interpreted as personally or professionally inappropriate.
- Assuming the role of staff advocate or sounding board for staff complaints.

Important Board Boundaries

Some personnel-oriented actions can actually put you and the organization at risk legally. So it's important to remember that:

- The chief executive typically handles and oversees staff performance reviews and termination decisions, not the board.

- Board members should refrain from communicating with any employee about personnel-related matters. If an employee reaches out to you or other board members regarding a personnel issue, it's best not to respond directly. Rather, notify the chief executive immediately, so it can be handled through the proper human resource channels.

- Most employment cases today involve damaging emails, texts or voicemails. Any such communications concerning personnel matters among board members, or from a board member to the chief executive or other staff, are discoverable in litigation, as are messages or postings on social media—even if you thought they were "private."

- If an attorney has been engaged to represent your organization, then direct communication with the attorney is typically protected by attorney-client privilege and is not discoverable. However, you'll want to clarify this fact before any communication takes place.

- During board meetings, personnel issues should only be discussed in a private executive session with just the chief executive present—no other staff. Board meeting notes should simply say "Private Personnel Matter," with no mention of the employee's name, as those notes are also discoverable.

Ultimately, as a leader of the organization, **you also have a great opportunity to help create a culture that both attracts and retains high-caliber personnel.** The way you interact with the organization's staff can make a big difference in the quality of their experience. By helping them feel recognized and appreciated, and by being a true partner in carrying out the organization's work, you bring out the best in everyone.

Important Tip:
It's a good idea for nonprofits to carry Directors' and Officers' (D&O) insurance in addition to general liability coverage. According to the Nonprofits Insurance Alliance, a good D&O policy should include broad coverage for all types of employment-related actions, including wrongful termination, harassment, discrimination, failure to hire, etc.

It is vital that board members understand the spirit of the strategic plan.

Strategic planning is not a *pro forma* exercise. It's an organized, efficient and systematic process for charting a course for strategic growth. When done well, it is the catalyst for taking your nonprofit to new levels of effectiveness, impact and success.

High-impact organizations have strategic plans.

As a board member, strategic planning is an opportunity for you to help shape the organization's future and guide your own involvement efforts. Given how fast the world is moving and changing, major strategic planning usually takes place about every three years, with ongoing check-ins and a formal annual plan update to make any strategic adjustments that may be needed.

Your role in strategic planning is to:

■ **Ensure that your organization has a plan.** A plan is essential, because it serves as the touchstone for key organizational decisions as well as the basis for staff work plans. A strategic plan (or business plan, as some like to call it) also provides evidence to funders that your organization has its act together — in other words, a clear destination and a roadmap for getting where it wants to be. Some funders actually *require* the organizations they fund to have a written strategic plan.

Ready to increase your organization's social impact?

It starts by engaging in an open, thoughtful and informed dialogue to answer some meaty questions:

- **What results are we committed to achieving?**

- **How will we achieve those results?**

- **What's needed to equip our organization to achieve those results?**

- **Realistically, what will achieving those results cost?**

- **How will we fund the costs?**

Once you've figured out and agreed to the answers, the key to success is holding yourselves accountable.

continued

Your role in strategic planning is to:

▪ **Support a process that is well-thought-out and inclusive.** Gone are the days when the board went off for a day or two, created a plan, blessed it and delivered it back to staff for implementation. Successful organizations know that the best strategic plans are the result of a well-structured process that includes both board members and key staff. Organizations with very large boards often create a planning task force that includes a mix of board members and staff who are charged with creating the draft plan, which is then brought to the entire board for input and vetting before approval. Depending on your organization's complexity and resources, it can be helpful to engage a consultant who possesses nonprofit expertise to help structure the process, conduct some of the research and analysis, facilitate the planning session(s) and assist with final plan development.

▪ **Help to avoid the "echo chamber."** Too many organizations rely solely on the opinions of board members and staff to inform their strategic plans. Often, a *Strengths, Weaknesses, Opportunities, Threats* (SWOT) analysis or a similar exercise is conducted at the onset of the planning process. The problem? The entire plan is based on insiders' perspectives, opinions and biases. The real power of the process happens when the blinders come off and a fresh, multi-dimensional view of the organization is brought to the table that combines board and staff perspectives with other timely and relevant data.

continued

Your role in strategic planning is to:

■ **Take a fresh, holistic look at your organization.** Gathering a solid body of information typically entails a structured process that includes analyzing financial and program data and trends, understanding the competitive and sector landscapes, and conducting interviews or surveys with priority stakeholders such as board, staff, clients, members, funders, collaborators and influencers. It's this holistic view that most often creates "Aha!" moments and surfaces bold new opportunities to increase the organization's impact.

■ **Engage in the planning process.** As a board member, you will be asked to approve the organization's strategic plan. So it clearly behooves you to play an active role in the planning process. You can do so by contributing your ideas through interviews and/or surveys, participating in planning sessions, serving on a dedicated planning task force, and providing periodic feedback as the plan evolves.

■ **Actively support the plan's implementation.** The work doesn't stop once the strategic plan is completed. In fact, that's when the real action begins. The board assumes an important role in helping to carry the plan forward. Highly effective boards take this charge seriously and ensure that each board member develops his or her own annual personal impact plan that aligns with the organization's strategic goals.

- **Model accountability.** A well-conceived strategic plan sets the stage and direction for measurable progress. Timely progress updates from staff to the board should be expected. It's equally important for the board to follow up with its members periodically to see how they are doing in relation to their personal impact plans, and to provide the support, encouragement and recognition that keeps everyone — staff and board members — focused, engaged and productive.

- **Evaluate and evolve.** As a board member, a recurring question in much of your decision-making should be, "How will doing this help us achieve the goals in our strategic plan?" A well-constructed plan provides a clear framework for evaluating and pursuing new opportunities — or for cutting bait on strategies that are no longer working. Having a plan doesn't mean you stop thinking or become rigid. It's essential to continuously gather and consider new internal and external data and information to make the strategic adjustments needed to maximize success.

An effective strategic or business plan is essential **for every nonprofit. It helps both the board as a whole, and you as an individual, to focus your energy and commitment on the areas where you can make the greatest difference.**

Excellent
board members

ensure that they don't spread themselves too thin when it comes to board service, either in terms of time or financial commitment.

MODEL **MEANINGFUL** GIVING.

Each organization sets it own expectations regarding how much fundraising involvement and financial support are expected of its board members.

At times, an eagerness to attract new board members causes organizations to downplay the role that they actually need board members to perform when it comes to personal giving and fundraising activities. The consequences of not being direct and transparent at the outset can make for uncomfortable dynamics down the road.

Some organizations clearly articulate a minimum give-or-get policy that all board members are expected to meet. Others state general expectations for board support but do not set a specific requirement. And there can be board positions and boards in which giving or raising funds is not an expectation, although these are less typical.

"Let's just raise more money from corporations and foundations."

Many board members are unaware that the majority of funds donated to nonprofits come from individuals rather than corporations or private foundations. In fact, in 2018, over two-thirds (68%) of the total charitable dollars received by nonprofits in the United States were contributed by individuals.

SOURCE: GIVING USA 2018,
THE ANNUAL REPORT ON PHILANTHROPY

Details are often required.

In the past, checking a box on a grant application indicating that the board actively gives was sufficient. Today, many funders require a more detailed overview that enables them to evaluate just how supportive the board really is.

So what does it mean to model meaningful giving?

By serving on a board, you're signaling that the organization is special to you. What's even more helpful to the organization is when this sentiment translates directly to your philanthropic priorities by placing it at, or near the top, of your commitments.

It's one thing to approach giving from a "meet the minimum" perspective. It's another to make it your practice to stretch a little or a lot...and give to your capacity in terms of financial support and actively helping raise support for the organization.

What you do personally – and what the board does collectively – matters.

- Your commitment to both "giving and getting" sends a powerful message and helps to set the bar for other board members.
- You become much more persuasive to potential supporters when you can authentically talk about why you've chosen to invest in the organization.
- The full participation of every board member confirms to corporate and foundation funders, as well as other important stakeholders, that the board is firmly behind the organization.

Bearing all this in mind, be sure you clearly understand your nonprofit's expectations before you pursue or accept a board position. Or if you're already on the board, and the expectations are fuzzy, perhaps you can be a catalyst for putting some structure in place.

Avoid getting a premature "NO."

Sometimes eager board members leave board or committee meetings ready to put the pedal to the metal. Before they've left the parking lot, they spontaneously begin hitting their speed dial. Unfortunately, when it comes to fundraising or securing a high-profile honoree or sponsor for an event, doing so can unintentionally and unnecessarily lead to a dead end.

Before you make any calls or send any emails or texts, collaborate with staff and other board members to think through a cultivation and solicitation approach that has the strongest potential to deliver a positive response. Together you'll determine:

- **Who** should be involved in approaching the prospective donor.

- **What** the person's history, ties or interests are that relate to your cause or organization.

- **How** to sequence the ask process.

- **When** the timing is right.

Say "YES!" to fundraising.

Among the many hats you wear as a board member is that of helping to grow the base of supporters for the organization. In fact, you could say it's the most impactful contribution you can make outside the boardroom.

Highly effective board members fully embrace being a public face for their organization and acting as ambassadors who raise awareness and build valuable relationships with individuals, businesses, foundations and the community. They don't view fundraising as an unsavory task that is relegated to staff or fellow board members. Rather, they view it as an opportunity to build connections with people who potentially have an interest in your organization's focus and mission.

Although it isn't always openly articulated, the bottom line is:

Yes, the vast majority nonprofits expect their board members to help with fundraising.

No, that doesn't mean they expect you to pester and beg your family, friends and colleagues for donations. No honorable organization wants you to be *that* pushy person.

Fundraising is not about hard-selling and arm-twisting. Rather, it's about **sharing your passion and helping others find a match for their philanthropic interests and passions.** Your cause and organization will be the right fit for some donors, and not for others.

A role for every board member

When it comes to fundraising, every single board member has a role to play. You just need to choose your lane and enjoy the ride.

Here's how: As part of creating your annual personal impact plan, work with your Board Chair, Chief Executive and/or Development Director to determine two things: (1) how much you're going to give personally; and (2) what role you will play in helping to raise support.

Ideally, your nonprofit has some supports in place to motivate and equip board members for success. These may include:

- **Board Training**: Aimed at building board members' communications and fundraising skills, including how to personalize and deliver a powerful elevator speech.
- **A Board Fundraising Engagement Model:** A simple structure that accommodates different styles, comfort levels, experience and skills. A solid model creates a clear on-ramp for board members by outlining specific expectations and clearly articulating their roles and responsibilities.

Successful fundraisers know that the task is multifaceted and requires an array of coordinated activities. As a board member, you can play one or more roles in that process...

Connectors

are enthusiastic about the organization and focus on building relationships. They help to spread the word and introduce people to your cause. Connectors are adept at delivering their elevator speech and talking about the organization. They invite people to take facility tours and attend events; they host gatherings; they help thank and steward relationships with current donors; and they proactively identify opportunities for your organization to increase its visibility. **All board members are Connectors.**

Builders

help establish and advance strong strategic relationships. They are well-versed in the organization's vision and strategic plan and can ably handle key questions. Their efforts are squarely aimed at laying the groundwork for investment. Builders accompany senior staff and fellow board members on calls or visits with current and prospective donors, policymakers, community leaders and other influencers.

Closers

play a significant role in the donor cultivation and solicitation process. They help surface and understand potential donors' priorities and interests and are comfortable making the "ask." Closers work hand-in-glove with the organization to develop donor strategies. They are called upon to write notes or letters, make personal phone calls, help shape proposals and meet face-to-face with donors for the purposes of making the request.

Helping to ensure that your organization has the resources to fulfill its mission can, without a doubt, be one of the most rewarding aspects of serving on the board. And having board members who own and master their Connector, Builder and Closer roles is an essential part of the equation.

When you describe your organization
to someone who is unfamiliar with it,
the response you are aiming for
is not a passive,
"Sounds like a good organization."

Rather, you're shooting for,

"Wow! Tell me more!"

Take your elevator speech to a higher level.

Board members often say they're stumped when asked to explain their nonprofit to others in a succinct and compelling way. The usual default is to rattle off a reference to its size or longevity, state its mission in a general way, or recite a laundry list of programs and services – all of which can quickly fall on politely deaf ears. The second default is to ask staff to provide a ready-made elevator speech to memorize. That typically falls flat, too.

Why? Because the magic in an elevator speech is the authentic and the unexpected – something that causes the listener to pause and think.

The fact is, you're not really making a speech. **You're giving people a glimpse into why this organization exists** in a way that is aimed at piquing their interest, opening the door to more conversation and, ultimately, gaining their engagement and support.

To make an elevator speech really sing, include an insight or proof point.

Neuroscientists can see it happening: People's brains light up when they are learning something new, are being prompted to see or do something differently, or are listening to an engaging story. You can trigger that response when you give a personal account of something valuable and unexpected that you have discovered about the organization. It can take the form of sharing a new insight you gained about an issue. Or you can offer a proof point: specific evidence of how the organization is having a positive impact on an important issue.

When these converge, an elevator speech can be immensely powerful. And that's when the perception of your organization shifts from doing "good work" to doing "essential work."

How to identify insights and proof points?

First, take a few moments to identify what makes the organization special to you. Then, thoughtfully consider a few things about how the organization is:

- Addressing an urgent and important unmet need
- Approaching an issue or problem in an innovative way
- Making a difference in the lives of individuals
- Having a tangible impact on a major issue

Keep asking yourself, "Why would this matter to the person I'm talking to?" Don't stop at the obvious; keep digging until you strike gold!

Constructing a Compelling Pitch

You can create a brief and powerful narrative for your organization using the following message framework:

Message	Example
Make it personal.	Every day I saw the same homeless family near my work, and one day one of the children reached out to me and touched my heart.
Share an insight.	What I didn't realize is that almost a quarter of the homeless people in our city are children, and some of their biggest struggles have to do with getting an education.
Make a distinction.	This organization is the only one in our area that focuses on helping homeless children get enrolled and stay in school.
Provide a proof point.	As a direct result of their efforts, last year more than a hundred homeless children in our community successfully completed a full year of school.
Offer an engagement. opportunity	They're having an event next week. Want to come along?

Can you get there in 30 seconds? **Yes, you can!**

Keep it current

Get in the habit of periodically taking stock of what to include in your elevator speech, for a few reasons:

Your messaging will stay in sync with the organization and where it's headed.

You'll continue to collect powerful stories and examples that can be used in conversations with others.

Best of all,

you'll regularly remind yourself of the organization's value and why you care about it. It's an excellent way to recharge your own enthusiasm and commitment!

Know Your Target. Tailor Your Message.

Your main focus may differ depending on your audience. For example, you may be:

- Educating people about a problem or need that they are not aware of.
- Explaining what differentiates your organization from others.
- Helping your audience see the possibilities for positive change and the consequences of inaction.

Regardless of the content of your elevator speech, it's always about conveying your commitment and enthusiasm for the organization in a way that kindles a spark in your listener.

EXCELLENCE

STRIVE FOR EXCELLENCE, NOT PERFECTION.

Excellence or perfection — why choose? Both excellence and perfection are admirable qualities. However, as it turns out, organizational psychologists have studied this topic extensively and concluded that the quest for perfection, while noble in theory, can create big stumbling blocks to getting things done in an organization.

It's worth taking a moment to reflect on this, because it defines a mindset that can increase your effectiveness as a board member.

EXCELLENCE

Here are a few telling comparisons:

Perfectionists	Excellence seekers
Set impossible goals	Set high and achievable goals
Are plagued by doubt	Are confident
Feel pressure	Feel excitement
Become overwhelmed and give up when they run into difficulty	Perceive setbacks as temporary and keep going
Are highly risk-averse	Are willing to take risks
Hate criticism and are devastated by failure	View criticism and failure as opportunities to learn
Need to have full control	Embrace spontaneity
Need to be "number one" — or else	Find fulfillment in trying their hardest

Most of us have witnessed situations in which the compulsion to make every detail perfect or to control for every unknown has stalled group momentum, built frustration and caused an organization to miss out on important opportunities.
Excellence, not perfection, holds the key.

EXCELLENCE

Seeking perfection is a solitary job.

Pursuing excellence is a way to invigorate a group.

As a board member, you can contribute to a culture of excellence; first, by putting your efforts into making sure that high standards are set and issues are thoughtfully considered; and second, by recognizing that you will never have all the answers but are continuously testing and learning along the way.

So, encourage your board to put its best foot forward and go!

Avoid Unintended Consequences.

Serving on a board can be a heady experience.
You're at the top, on the inside. As historians and observers of human nature throughout time have told us, an unintended consequence of gaining power is its potential to elevate the ego and bring out a subtle (or not-so-subtle) sense of entitlement.

While the odds are low that you joined your board aspiring to be a supreme dictator or to have your ego stroked, it's deceptively easy to adopt habits or behaviors that subconsciously work against the true spirit of supporting your nonprofit.

A few self-serving scenarios to avoid:

Viewing the board as your personal soapbox.

No matter how passionate or informed you are about an issue, a board meeting is not the place to pontificate. You and your colleagues will find it far more helpful to approach meetings with the goal of contributing your insights thoughtfully and efficiently to achieve the established agenda.

Siphoning off resources for pet projects.

It's true that an enthusiastic champion is often key to a project or activity's success. Yet, there can be pitfalls. A classic example is the tradition of a board president setting a theme or focus area for the year. Too often, the type of project that results is more of a "one-off" than an opportunity to put more muscle into achieving a mission-critical goal. So take care that whatever idea you put forth or embrace is firmly aligned with the organization's goals and strategic priorities.

Consuming significant, often scarce, resources.

It can be extremely valuable to take a realistic look at how much of your organization's human and financial resources are spent supporting governance functions. In long-established nonprofits, it's not uncommon for the board, committees and task forces to balloon in size, becoming disproportionally heavy consumers of the organization's resources.

What often goes unrecognized is the staff time and resources that are required for every meeting, whether virtual or face-to-face: arranging logistics, juggling multiple schedules, creating.background materials and talking points, prepping for presentations and conducting post-meeting follow-up. In addition, in-person meetings often entail direct costs for travel, lodging and food.

So before recommending yet another meeting or committee, think carefully about whether it is truly justified. You may find that simply by asking the question, you and your fellow board members may arrive at a better and more efficient way to advance an issue or project.

Balancing board perks

One of the key ways organizations demonstrate appreciation for their board members is by holding meetings or retreats in enjoyable settings, offering interesting activities that facilitate relationship-building or giving tokens of appreciation to board members. These are usually heartfelt gestures, and it's appropriate to accept them graciously. Just make sure you and your fellow board members are doing your part to ensure that things don't become too extravagant.

Steer Clear of Conflicts of Interest

As a best practice, an organization should have an articulated conflict-of-interest policy. By definition, a conflict of interest is a transaction or arrangement that might benefit the private interest of an officer, board member or employee. A common example is when a board member runs a business that sells something the organization might need and has a chance to influence the purchasing decision. Or the organization might be considering hiring a board member's relative. In both cases, a policy would require the board member to recuse themself from voting on any purchasing, hiring or compensation-related decisions.

Many other potential conflict-of-interest scenarios are less obvious. Often, such situations can occur because a well-meaning board member is attempting to do a favor for the organization. It's always best to bring attention to any gray area up front, and seek expert counsel to ensure that you and your organization don't inadvertently get into trouble.

Think before you post

Social media is a powerful way for board members to help amplify visibility for the nonprofit they serve. Before doing so, it's important to understand the ground rules. **Why?** Because in both the real and digital worlds, organizations can be held responsible for the actions of their volunteers.

Often, scenarios that lead to trouble are innocent and well-intended.

- **Suppose you're volunteering at an event** involving your nonprofit's clients and you take some great photos of the smiling children enjoying the activities. Then, you post those photos on your personal social media page. What you didn't know is some of the children are under court supervision and cannot legally be featured in photographs. Suddenly, your nonprofit is in serious hot water.

- **Or, you've identified yourself online as a board member** of a nonprofit and you're well-known in the community for that role. There's a hotly contested election season and you regularly voice your opinions and candidate endorsements. It can get tricky quickly because organizations that hold section 501(c)(3) tax exemptions are strictly prohibited from engaging in any political activity. So, any impression that you're speaking on behalf of the organization, even if unintentional, could be a problem.

- **The best way to avoid sticky situations** is to err on the side of caution and restraint. And, don't hesitate to ask your organization to provide guidelines and training, so you can use your social media with confidence on its behalf.

"Life expands or shrinks in proportion to one's courage."

ANAÏS NIN

COURAGE.
BRING IT!

Leading an organization in today's hypercompetitive, rapidly changing world is not for the faint of heart. **It takes courage to face facts,** identify challenges and do something about them — especially if that means adopting bold, new approaches that break with long-held mindsets or traditions.

Courageous leadership means understanding and confronting realities, not denying them or putting off facing and addressing them. It means being willing to ask honest, open questions, gather objective data, and challenge "what we've always done" in the context of what genuinely needs to change, to ensure that the organization fulfills its purpose.

There's a crucial difference

between bravery and courage.

While the brave take risks

and plunge into the unknown

without hesitation,

the courageous fully understand

the risks before them and

mindfully take action anyway,

despite their fears, in order to

achieve an end they believe in.

A courageous leader fully claims his or her leadership roles and responsibilities while fostering a culture of respect and collaboration. A courageous leader also recognizes that there are times when difficult or even unpopular decisions must be made and is willing to take on the uncomfortable task of leading the organization through them. As mistakes are inevitably made, it takes another dose of courage to avoid pointing the finger at others, and instead accept responsibility, regroup and forge ahead.

Courage-infused leadership isn't always pretty, but the rewards are great. Courageous leadership builds credibility and trust. When you are recognized as a person of character, it's easy for others to believe in you and your cause.

By your willingness to serve on a board, you've shown that you are committed to making a difference. At times, that will mean digging deep and finding the courage to do what it takes to help transform the organization.

"If we were supposed to talk
more than we listen,
we would have two tongues
and one ear."

MARK TWAIN

Listen up!

How many times have you waited impatiently for a fellow board member to stop talking so you can make your point? It happens all the time in board meetings, especially if the topic is highly charged or hotly debated.

We often overlook what someone is saying because **we're busy formulating a response.** Or as Stephen R. Covey notes in *The 7 Habits of Highly Effective People,* "Most people do not listen with the intent to understand; they listen with the intent to reply."

The eye roll.
The tapping foot.
The heavy sigh.

If you're guilty of one or all of these, you're sending a clear message to the person who's speaking: "I'm finished listening to you." Regardless of what they're saying or how they're saying it, be mindful of the message you're conveying as you listen. Everyone has his or her own opinions and individual manner of speaking. The boardroom is the perfect place to model respect and good listening skills.

Are you a sentence-grabber?

When impatience takes over, it's tempting to try to speed things along by interrupting a speaker or finishing others' sentences. Beyond disrupting the flow of information, the "interrupter" is following his or her own train of thought, squelching the opportunity to learn where the speaker was originally headed — and possibly sabotaging a great idea.

The International Listening Organization estimates that we listen at the rate of 125-250 words a minute, but we think at 1,000-3,000 words a minute. With all those words vying for attention in our brains, it's a wonder we hear anything at all. By giving more air time to the words in our head than the ones entering our ears, we run the risk of missing something important, even vital. Turning down our own inner dialogue allows us to listen more carefully and stay focused on the issue at hand.

The ability to give our full attention to what someone is saying is a profoundly important skill for board members. It takes practice, and isn't always easy. Being a good listener helps avoid misunderstandings and makes decision-making processes flow more smoothly. Good listening reinforces trust, strengthens relationships and makes a board's work more efficient, productive and meaningful.

Genuine listening not only helps everyone better understand a situation or issue; it will help you and your fellow board members get the firmest possible grip on the best ways to address your organization's needs.

When your board is diverse, you're in excellent company!

Social physics research by MIT's Media Lab and other studies reveal that groups with a mix of ages, genders and cultural backgrounds regularly come up with more effective and feasible solutions than those that are homogeneous.

There's more to diversity than meets the eye.

Diversity has a multitude of facets — some we're born with, some we've picked up along the way – and they all help to define us. Every individual brings a rich combination of assets to the table. Common traits and experiences can be the basis for bonding, while those that are different have the potential to expand one's thinking.

As a board member, it's critical to remember that diversity goes far beyond the observable demographics of age, gender, race and ethnicity. The term also applies to all of the possibilities along the various dimensions of occupation, educational background, income, religious and political beliefs, hometown, sexual orientation/gender identity, marital and parental status, and so on.

Diversity is our reality.

By nearly any measure, we live in a world defined by diversity. One indicator: As recently as 1990, the U.S. population was more than 75 percent Caucasian. However, those born after 1996 now comprise the first majority-minority generation in our history, in which no ethnic group approaches 50 percent. This cohort fully expects to be immersed in diversity and views anything else as off-kilter.

SOURCE: US CENSUS BUREAU

Millennials are getting on board!

One of the most highly touted traits of the Millennial generation is their commitment to community service. There are indications that this value is carrying over into their adult life: In 2019 we conducted a study of the volunteer activities of over 600 alumni of a major California university and found that 36% of those who graduated in the past 10 years are already serving on a nonprofit board, and another 45% are planning to do so within the next 5 years.

How do excellent board members think about diversity?

They proactively seek it and embrace it. There's a growing body of evidence that considering diverse points of view not only leads to more creative and innovative thinking, but richer relationships. Staying within familiar boundaries requires minimal effort; it's the challenge of seeing and understanding things through different lenses that stimulates new insights and deeper connections. That principle definitely holds true when it comes to board recruitment. Making an intentional effort to reach beyond the usual circles to bring together a spectrum of cultural, age, gender and professional backgrounds can prove enormously valuable when tackling the complex issues facing today's nonprofits.

They recognize that not everyone hears or see things the same way. Different cultures instill their own norms of etiquette. Even words and expressions may mean different things to different people. Taking time to identify and learn about these nuances is a great way to show respect, develop empathy and broaden one's own horizons.

They resist falling into the habit of overgeneralizing. Broad assumptions surface in boardrooms all the time – for instance, when a board member turns to a Hispanic colleague and asks how Catholics feel about an issue, never considering that might not be that person's religion. While it is appropriate to consider the cultural context of your fellow board members, at the same time it's essential to avoid stereotyping and assuming all members of a particular group feel and act exactly the same way.

"Diversity is the art
of thinking independently
together."

MALCOLM FORBES

Each recognizes that he or she is not the sum of their demographic. If you're the only person under 30 in the room, resist the temptation to speak as the definitive voice for your entire generation. While you certainly have useful insights, the way you really add value is by helping your colleagues see distinctions they might miss and connecting them with others in your age group who can expand their experience.

They strive to keep an open mind and avoid judging or dismissing other perspectives. They also recognize that everyone, including themselves, has built-in biases of their own. As author and philosopher Anais Nin observed, "We don't see things as they are. We see them as *we* are."

They get more data when it's needed. An anecdote or two about a particular group, no matter how compelling, does not a trend make. To identify real trends or shifts in the social or cultural landscape, you need a broader perspective. When key strategic decisions are being contemplated, it's critical that you use good, objective data obtained from key audiences outside the boardroom.

Alphabet-soup acronyms and jargon plague most nonprofits. As a board member, it's important for you to take ownership by learning what all those letters stand for. You might suggest that staff maintain a working "code list" of key terms to help everyone stay on the same page.

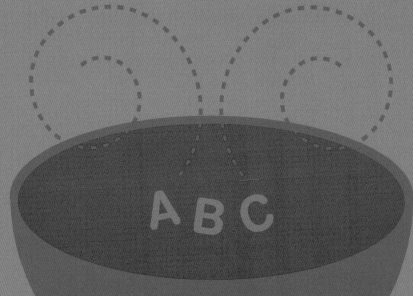

Do your homework.

It's always challenging to find your balance among work, home and volunteer activities. And without a doubt, adding "board member" to your list of roles includes a certain amount of outside-the-boardroom homework. It's a very real part of the job.

In advance of each board meeting, staff typically work diligently to prepare and distribute board packets that give all the detailed information you'll need to participate in focused deliberations, pose insightful questions and arrive at sound decisions.

So read them!

Too often, reviewing pre-meeting materials can become a last-minute exercise — sometimes so last-minute that you're literally sitting in the room just seconds before the meeting begins before you crack open the packet and furiously thumb through it.

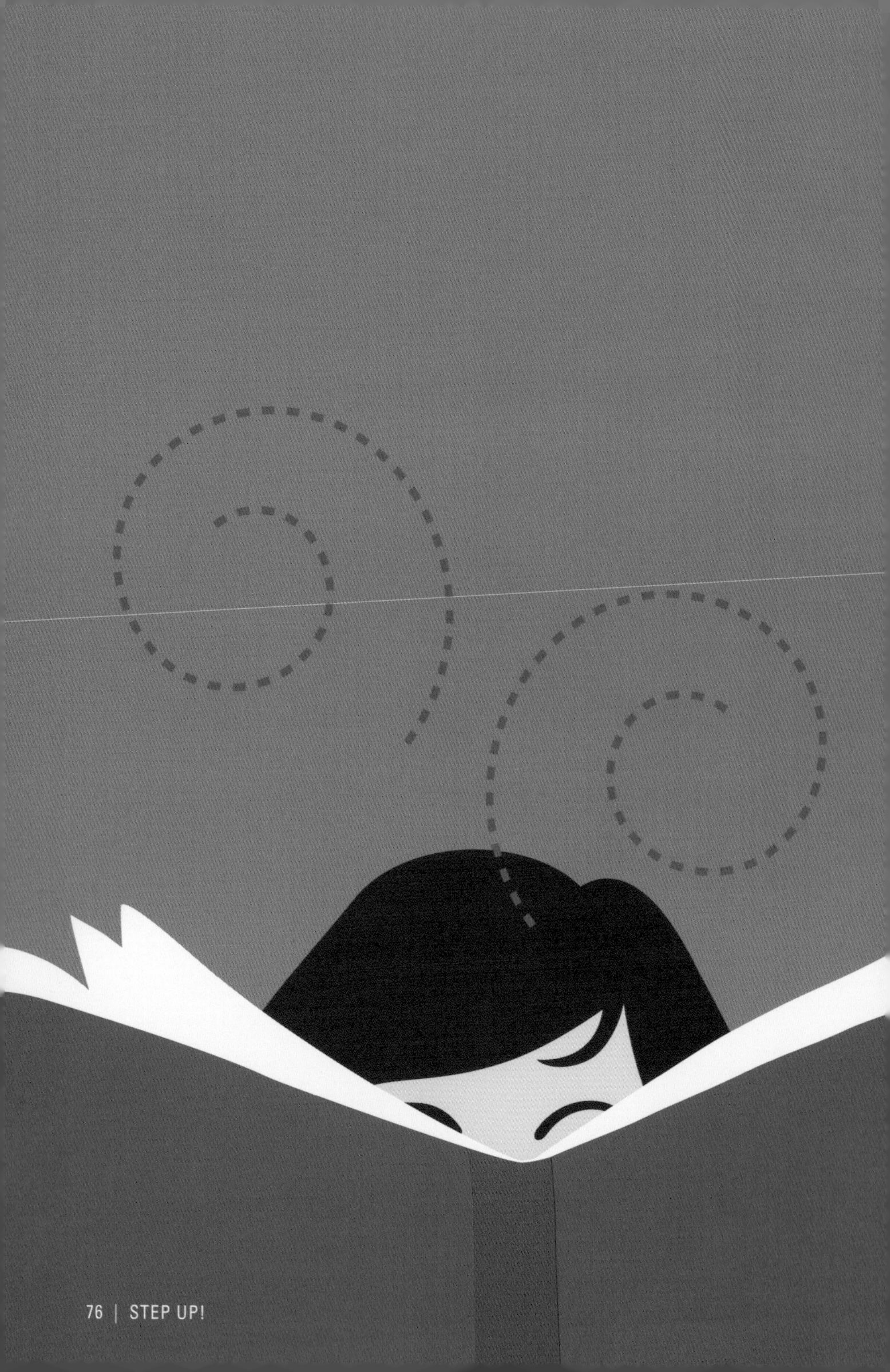

Those who do not take the time to review information thoughtfully before a meeting often find themselves in a precarious position: They either bog down the meeting by asking questions about topics that are clearly covered in the materials; or their embarrassment at being unprepared gets the best of them, and they blindly vote with the majority. Neither does justice to your role or the organization.

Here's another benefit to advance preparation: Say you have received information ahead of time, but you aren't sure how to read and interpret a financial report or some other component. Excellent! Now you have time before the meeting to reach out and get clarification from staff, so you **come to the meeting confident, prepared and ready to move the organization forward.**

Avoid the three Ds: Distraction, Disruption, Downer.

It's the little things that can wreak havoc on group dynamics and derail meetings. Recognizing and steering clear of behaviors that undermine your board's effectiveness and send meetings careening into the ditch is a responsibility that each board member can and should fully own.

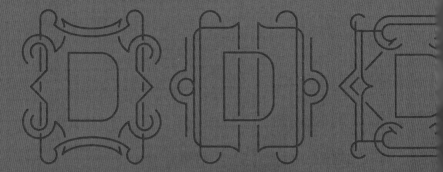

Brain research shows **that**

if you lead with a positive statement,

your comments stand a much better

chance of being accepted by others.

"THE NEUROCHEMISTRY OF POSITIVE CONVERSATIONS,"
BY JUDITH GLASER AND RICHARD GLASER,
HARVARD BUSINESS REVIEW, 2014.

So when possible, start by noting an aspect of the idea you genuinely like. If that's not feasible, you can express your appreciation of the work that has gone into researching the topic, or how important you think it is to bring ideas to the table. From there, you can air specific questions or concerns. The goal is to arrive at a solution that works, not simply to reject what's being discussed and considered.

Distractors engage in sidebar conversations, constantly check their email or mobile devices, or do something other than actively listen and participate in the meeting.

It's one thing to make a friendly aside or comment to the person next to you. Just make it quietly, and keep it brief. Conducting a full-on conversation, searching online to validate or invalidate something that has been said means you're actually conducting a separate meeting.

Disrupters lob toxic, verbal grenades into the boardroom. Their vehemently stated opinions suck the energy out of the room, put people on the defensive, and can make some feel too intimidated to speak up. This is especially true if the boardroom bully or know-it-all is a longtime member, and others are new to the scene.

> **"That's the stupidest idea I've ever heard."**
> **"That will never work."**
> **"Sheesh... We tried this a few years ago,**
> **and it failed miserably. Why are we wasting**
> **time on it now?"**

When statements are loaded with emotion and delivered with authority, those who feel less strongly may refrain from voicing their own more balanced opinions. On the other hand, those who also disagree may join in with equally incendiary, counterproductive remarks. Dominating a meeting is a surefire way to shut down honest input and discussion.

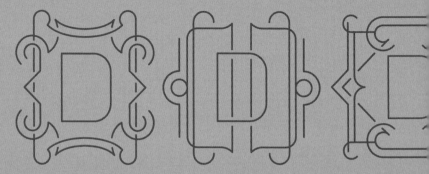

How to address

bullying in the boardroom

- It all starts with good board training. Establish solid ground rules for group discussions, including the maximum amount of time for individual comments on a topic.

- Reinforce that the Board Chair's job is to ensure that all opinions are heard and to uphold time limits.

- Underscore that board decision-making is a collaborative process, and while disagreements may occur, they need to be handled respectfully.

- If a discussion gets too heated, call for a short break, regroup and convey a plan for either completing the agenda item during that board meeting or in a subsequent meeting.

- If you sense that a board member is generally upset or unhappy and is taking out their frustration in the boardroom, schedule a one-on-one meeting with them and the Board Chair and possibly the chief executive to better understand their perspective and to determine if a resolution is possible.

- If the board member continues to display disruptive behavior, removing that person from the board may be necessary.

Downers make being critical or playing devil's advocate their default mode. Their first instinct is to "go to the dark side" and reject an idea out-of-hand. Instead of considering positive possibilities, their primary focus is to reveal why something doesn't or won't work.

Downers may position themselves as the voice of reason, possessed of superior experience or organizational knowledge. It can become part of their identity to believe that, by taking on the role of resident critic, they are serving as a "protector" of the organization.

Even well-intentioned actions of this type can stymie a group's ability to engage in meaningful discussion, productively challenge conventional thinking or contribute ideas and solutions.

What to do about a really bad idea?

If you think an idea is flawed, you have a responsibility to speak up. But resist the urge to blurt out a scathing criticism. It will make a difference if you pause, breathe deeply and take a moment to frame your thoughts. Make it your job to bring positive energy into the boardroom.

NO ELEPHANTS
OR COWS.

"Are we going to talk about
the elephant in the room?"

Given organizational histories and multiple stakeholders,
**nonprofits can be fertile ground for invisible elephants
and sacred cows.** Both become particularly problematic in
the boardroom, where a put-everything-on-the-table mode of
operating is essential to ensure that the organization focuses
resources on what matters most and supports activities that
truly deliver a solid return on investment.

Adhering to a

no-elephants-and-sacred-cows

policy plays an important role in

maintaining a board culture

that fosters open communication

and creative problem-solving.

It's not uncommon for research or a strategic-planning process to turn up activities or organizational artifacts that are out of alignment with the organization's mission or are draining resources in ways that are disproportionate to the value they deliver. For example, governance structures and processes may have become unwieldy. Pet programs may have continued "just because." Other activities may still be in place despite declining interest and usage. Or there may be unspoken, unresolved situations that are coloring everyone's ability to think objectively about matters at hand.

It can feel personal. A sacred cow could be something that is truly beloved by a handful of tenured and respected leaders or a subgroup of constituents. The "elephant in the room" could be a major initiative that is not succeeding as expected. Shifting strategy or cutting bait can be complicated, even embarrassing. However, regardless of the situation or scenario, ignoring the issue will do nothing to help the organization.

"If you always do

what you've always done,

you'll always get

what you've always got."

HENRY FORD

In truth, being timid in the boardroom can have serious repercussions. By the time the sense of urgency builds to a level where the group can't avoid raising questions or suggesting that something needs to change it can be too late — after the organization has already slid into crisis mode or missed important opportunities. Attempting to manage sensitive issues from a defensive or reactive position almost always results in damaged relationships and less-than-desired outcomes.

How to contend with these animals?

The first step is to make it safe to bring them out into the open. Any board member can set that in motion, starting with something as simple as an acknowledgment that every organization has them, and that it's part of the work of the board to look at them periodically with clear, custodial eyes. Doing so opens the door for proactive discussions that can be handled in a respectful manner that honors past decisions while staying focused on making whatever changes are called for, and keeps the organization relevant and successfully moving forward.

"Where all think alike,
no one thinks very much."

WALTER LIPPMANN

"Honest disagreement
is often a good sign of progress."

MOHANDAS K. GANDHI

CONFLICT
IS NOT A DIRTY WORD.

There are lots of reasons why we are conditioned to shy away from conflict in a group. Conflict can make us uncomfortable. It can feel hostile. It's perceived to create winners and losers. It can cause rifts that damage relationships. **For most people, conflict sits on the opposite side of fun;** people regularly describe themselves as being conflict-averse.

Yet, in groups of diverse people with passionately held beliefs and opinions, **conflict is both natural and inevitable.** In fact, it is often through conflict — or working through differing beliefs and opinions — that some of the biggest, most promising opportunities emerge.

As a board member, how do you deal most effectively with "Conflict"?

Expect conflict and recognize the valuable potential it holds. When you sense dissension coming, remember that allowing deep-seated feelings to surface can create the opportunity to air issues that may be holding back the work of the board. By dispensing with superficial politeness and directly addressing differences, you can reach new levels of honesty, trust and relationship-building.

Be prepared for it. Make sure you understand the protocol for how your board handles serious differences of opinion. Whose role is it to take charge? What processes are in place to make sure the issue is managed respectfully and productively? If a clear, transparent process doesn't exist, consider suggesting that the board articulate one.

Be curious. Before you jump in with a vocal opinion or dig in your heels, challenge yourself to explore what different pieces of information or experiences may be contributing to the disparate perspectives around the table. This is your chance to gain valuable knowledge and show genuine interest in other vantage points and, at the same time, help diffuse emotions.

Use your insights to arrive at a new and better place together. "Compromise" is not a dirty word, either. In fact, it's usually the key to productive conflict resolution. Considering multiple possibilities and encouraging divergent thinking builds the muscles that can help your board become a more finely-tuned working team that is not only able to make effective day-to-day decisions, but capable of coming up with breakthrough ideas.

Another big C is "Confidentiality."

It's almost always harmful when board members take a debate outside the boardroom. When tough situations arise, agree as a group on what to say, what not to say, and to whom. When in doubt, err on the side of discretion.

Boards only have
authority as a group,
not as individuals.

Stand as one.

Boards exist in part to make substantive decisions,
from setting an organization's strategic direction and goals to
hiring the chief executive and approving the annual budget.
In each case, boards are called upon to review, deliberate and
arrive at informed decisions that align with and support the
organization's mission.

Although a board is composed of individuals, it only has
authority as a group. **Each and every board member
is bound by the decisions that the board makes
collectively.**

It's expected that not every decision will receive unanimous
approval and support. In fact, there may be heated debates
and strong opposing positions. However, once an issue
receives the required votes to approve it, kill it, or send it
back for further review, it becomes a decision that the entire
board must own.

What happens

in the boardroom

stays in the

boardroom.

When opinions differ, deliberations need to occur within the structure of the board rather than outside it. It can be extremely damaging to an organization for board members to air their dissatisfaction or concerns to stakeholders, staff or the media. Regrettably, individuals sometimes attempt to justify rogue actions as a personal "CYA" strategy, to warn someone about what's happening, or to lay the groundwork for an I-told-you-so moment. Being publicly at odds with collective board decisions, including having off-the-record discussions with staff or others, is almost never in the best interest of the organization, and it can actively undermine the chief executive's ability to lead effectively.

Tough decisions come with the territory. Inevitably, you may find yourself opposed to a group decision. If the issue is big enough, it may be the catalyst for you to reassess your participation on the board. More likely, it will be an opportunity for you to stretch your leadership skills to view and understand the issue from a different perspective.

You can take heart in the fact that many who study organizations agree with management expert Ken Blanchard, who states: **"None of us is as smart as all of us."** And regardless of the circumstance, it is each board member's obligation to uphold confidentiality, to make decisions collectively and to speak with one voice.

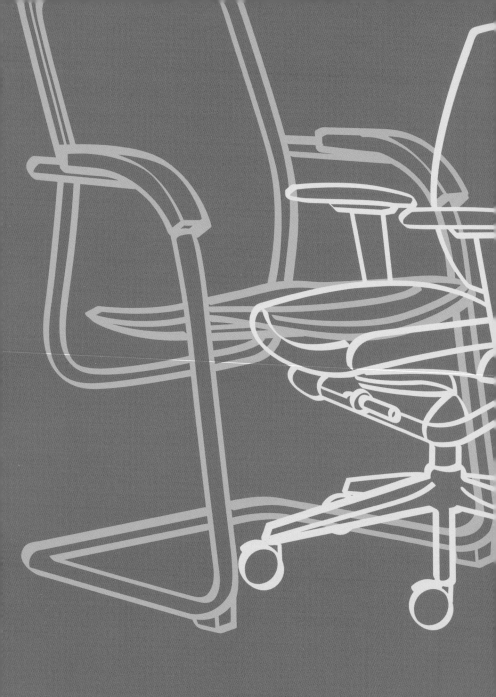

When you change seats,

YOUR ROLE CHANGES, TOO.

Way to go! You've stepped up and have become the board chair, or you've agreed to head up a key committee or task force.

If this is a new role for you, the shift may feel a little unsettling at first.

Chances are, you're in this new leadership position because you've proved to be an engaged and effective board member with a passion for the mission, a strong personality and a penchant for getting things done.

That's all good. However, in this new position, your primary job is no longer to be your vocal, persuasive self. Instead, you are being called upon to manage the group's process. That means it's your responsibility to ensure that everyone is heard, that ideas and solutions are vetted and the work of the group gets done.

Create a board meeting that YOU would want to attend.

■ **Take care of business.** Meaty topics should be slotted early in the agenda.

■ **Expand knowledge and understanding.** Include programming by staff or outside experts that provides interesting and important insights into your organization's sector, a particular program or area of focus, or how-to's to help your board perform at its highest level.

■ **Inspire and motivate.** Feature real examples and authentic stories that highlight the difference the organization is making in the lives of those you serve. And always recognize and celebrate progress!

For someone who is used to being an active player, it takes some discipline to think of yourself as a facilitator, in charge of running a productive meeting. It also means thinking a few steps ahead to make sure everything moves along smoothly. To accomplish this, a little preparation goes a long way.

Work with the chief executive and staff to prepare a thoughtful and strategic agenda. Clearly identify the decisions that need to be made or the actions that need to be taken. Determine where gaps may exist in the board's understanding of key topics. Anticipate questions. Make sure everyone has the necessary facts and context to make informed decisions. Build in time to recognize "wins" and progress. And remember to include a "mission moment" to help people stay connected to the meaningful work you're helping to accomplish.

You'll be glad you took the time to help inform the agenda, because an effective chairperson can truly make the difference between productive, successful, inspiring meetings and those that are a frustrating waste of time.

It's your responsibility to ensure
that everyone is heard, that ideas and solutions are vetted and that the work of the group gets done.

What will your legacy be?

As author and educator Steven Covey advises,
"Begin with the end in mind."
Embrace the organization's strategic vision and direction,
and make some personal goals as you start out
that reflect the impact you would like to make
both during and after your board tenure.

Make a graceful exit.

No matter how distant it may feel now, the day will come when your service on the board is at an end.

In the best case, leaving the board is part of the normal course of events, with your term clearly delineated and ending on schedule.

Or your departure could be precipitated by internal or external events. Perhaps a substantive change has occurred within the organization that you're unable to stand behind. Or you've dug deep and determined that, while worthy, the organization isn't honestly at or near the top of your volunteer commitment priorities. Maybe something in your personal or professional life is driving the need for a change.

Whatever leads up to that moment, you can do a lot to orchestrate a positive transition for both you and the organization by applying a few basic principles:

- Do some advance planning.
- Be honest and transparent.
- Show courtesy and respect.

Be gracious.

Regardless of the circumstances, take the high road.
Express your gratitude and liberally extend compliments for
whatever you have found to be positive about your board
experience. Include as many people as you authentically can.

Facilitate a smooth handoff.

Create a transition plan for any activities you are leading
or for which you carry major responsibility. If you chair a
committee, or play a key role in specific events or activities,
provide your successor with the background, documents, plans
and budgets needed to carry it forward. If possible, personally
brief whoever will be taking on the tasks. Stay engaged until
the end, and actively participate in whatever formal process
has been established for wrapping up your service, helping to
identify and recruit your successor, or whatever is called for
through your board's protocol.

Share what you've learned.

Your reflections on your experience can be very useful
for those who will carry the organization forward. A good
practice is for organizations to conduct exit interviews
with departing board members. The formal, confidential
setting of this conversation affords a perfect opportunity to
provide candid feedback and constructive suggestions. If the
organization doesn't have such a process in place, consider
initiating a call or meeting with the chief executive and the
appropriate board leader.

If you want to stay involved – find a way!

Board members know more about the organization than the vast majority of its constituents ever will. You're family. Former board members are often some of the organization's most persuasive, effective ambassadors and supporters long after their official board service has come to a close. **Making it known that you are eager and willing to continue to play a meaningful role will make your exit all the more graceful and positive.**

"I've learned that
people will forget what you said,
people will forget what you did,
but people will never forget
how you made them feel."

MAYA ANGELOU

Being proactive is far better **than having someone else, however gently and diplomatically, ask you to bow out.** If you sense that you are not living up to your board responsibilities, it's likely that others have noticed too. Rather than staying in that uncomfortable void, take the initiative. Have a conversation with the chief executive and appropriate board leaders to determine the best possible course of action.

When a mid-course departure is called for...

Regardless of the reason, there are some ways to create a softer landing for yourself and everyone involved:

- **Make an honest assessment.** Identify the factors that are in play, and whether they are creating a short-term situation or a long-term problem. Then thoughtfully consider the pros and cons of staying – both for your own good and the good of the organization.

- **As early as possible, involve the chief executive and appropriate board leaders.** Let them know what you are dealing with and get their perspectives on how best to handle things. Maybe you can continue in a modified way. Perhaps you need to phase out immediately or over a defined period. Or there might be another solution that you haven't thought of on your own.

- **Recognize how difficult it can be to let go of something you care about and probably enjoy.** That's where it helps to let your loyalty to the organization come to the forefront, and make it your priority to do whatever is in its best interest.

GO
ALL
IN

What should you do now? **GO ALL IN.**

If you're going to make the most of your board service, this is no time to hold back. In that spirit, here are a few ideas:

- **Transform your passion for the cause into full-on enthusiasm for the organization.** People often connect with a cause first and an organization second. Try reshuffling that order, and recognize that focusing your energies on building a thriving organization can actually help advance the cause in which you believe, in far more substantial and sustainable ways than you could accomplish on your own.

- **Stretch beyond your comfort zone.** Be on the lookout for opportunities in which your talents, experience and connections can make a difference, including those that may lie beyond your usual wheelhouse.

- **Make every minute count.** Time is your most precious and limited commodity. So don't just spend it; invest it with intention and purpose where it will yield the biggest returns.

- **Walk your talk.** Being a board member sends a public signal that the organization is deeply important to you. Giving to your capacity — in both time and financial resources — elevates your credibility as well as your impact.

In a nutshell...

Show up.

Never give up.

And whenever

the opportunity

presents itself –

STEP UP!

More Resources and Support

It's an exciting time in the nonprofit sector and a lot of great work is being done. We're committed to helping organizations and their leaders soar.

Visit our website, 2Bcommunications.com for free information and tools including a "Personal Impact Plan" template and other Step Up! handouts and resources.

Or email us at info@2bcommunications.com with any questions or thoughts. We'd love to hear your stories and insights as we continue on this important journey together.